Instant Novels

CREATIVE CHAPTER TITLES
Grades 4-6

Written by David Clark Yeager
Illustrated by Beverly Armstrong

The Learning Works

Edited by Sherri M. Butterfield

The purchase of this book entitles the individual teacher to reproduce copies for use in the classroom.

The reproduction of any part for an entire school or school system or for commercial use is strictly prohibited.

No form of this work may be reproduced or transmitted or recorded without written permission from the publisher.

Contents

Creating Classroom Novels

Instant Novels is a unique collection of twenty story starters designed to become first chapters in novels that students write. These story starters are classified into four distinct categories: science fiction, adventure, mystery, and awesome tales. Each story starter is approximately a page in length; and all of them end on a suspenseful note. Accompanying each one is a list of suggested titles for the nine additional chapters that are needed to complete the novel.

Working in groups of nine or fewer, students should select and read one of these first-chapter novel starters, and then create and record an appropriate title for it on the chapter title sheet. Next, they should decide who will write each one of the nine additional chapters and record their names on the chapter title sheet beside the appropriate chapter numbers and titles.

Encourage writing groups to brainstorm and record ideas about character, action, and setting. Writer's Worksheet 1 (on page 6) will help young authors organize these ideas and begin to develop a vocabulary that is appropriate to a particular time, place, and set of events. Writer's Worksheet 2 (on page 7) will help authors plan the action that is to take place in their chapters and become conscious of how their chapters fit with the rest of the novel, advancing the plot and contributing to the overall purpose.

After a comprehensive plan has been made and ideas have been shared, students should work independently, with a partner, or in small groups to create the chapters they have agreed to write. These chapters should be approximately 150 to 300 words in length. Each individual author or group of authors should retain the setting mentioned in the first chapter, continue the basic story line established there, and involve at least some, if not all, of the characters introduced in the first chapter in the action that takes place in subsequent chapters.

Creating Classroom Novels
(continued)

Before students begin to write, encourage them to do research that will acquaint them with the time period, particular place, and/or special events on which the novel is based so that they can provide factual background for the fiction they create. For example, students choosing to write chapters for *The Lost Continent* (pages 24–25) may need to learn more about continents (geography), movements of the earth's crust (geology), and differing theories about Atlantis, which place it in the Atlantic Ocean and in the Mediterranean Sea, before they begin their work. Likewise, students choosing to write chapters for *A Night in Pompeii* (pages 46–47) may need to learn more about archaeology; volcanoes; the circumstances surrounding the eruption of Mount Vesuvius on August 24, A.D. 79; exactly where Pompeii was located; what life in this ancient Italian town was like; and the circumstances surrounding its discovery in 1763, nearly seventeen hundred years after it had been buried beneath layers of cinder and ash.

After students have written their chapters, encourage them to meet together again to critique and edit their work, making whatever changes are necessary to correct spelling and punctuation errors, smooth transitions, improve continuity, standardize style, and make treatment of names and terms consistent throughout.

After the chapters have been written and edited, students can bind them into a book by following the instructions on page 48. Then, they can illustrate their novels and display them in the classroom for classmates to read and parents to enjoy.

Writer's Worksheet 1

Use this worksheet to organize your ideas about the characters, action, and setting of your novel and to begin to develop the vocabulary you will use in your novel.

Main Characters

Name	Title, Identification, or Brief Description
_____	_____
_____	_____
_____	_____
_____	_____
_____	_____

Action (that is, what happens in your novel)

_____

_____

Verbs That Might Be Used to Express This Action

_____	_____
_____	_____
_____	_____

Setting (that is, where the action takes place)

_____

Adjectives That Might Be Used to Describe This Setting

_____	_____
_____	_____
_____	_____

Writer's Worksheet 2

Use this worksheet to plan the action that will take place in your chapter.

1. What is the title of this chapter? _____

2. How did the preceding chapter end? _____
   _____

3. How will this chapter begin? _____
   _____

4. What will be the opening sentence of this chapter? _____
   _____

5. What goal will your main character try to achieve in this chapter? _____
   _____
   _____

6. How will he or she achieve this goal? _____
   _____

7. How will this chapter end? _____
   _____

8. What will be the closing sentence of this chapter? _____
   _____

9. Outline or summarize the action that will take place in this chapter.
   _____
   _____
   _____
   _____
   _____

10. How might the next chapter begin? _____
    _____

Professor Templeton's Time Machine

Chapter One

"At last! I have finished at last!" Professor Templeton exclaimed. "This is the greatest moment in my life."

David Lennon, the professor's most recent assistant, walked across the room and looked at the machine. "What's finished?" he asked.

"Why, the TTM-6, of course," the professor replied. "The Templeton Time Machine will revolutionize travel across the universe. If it works, of course."

"Of course," David replied, scratching his head. "Excuse me, Professor, but what exactly is the TTM-6?"

The professor rolled his eyes. "Why, it's the Templeton Time Machine. We'll be able to sell these little babies for a quarter of a million at least. Once you have proved it works, of course."

"Of course," David gulped nervously as he climbed into the time machine. "I have just one question, Professor."

Professor Templeton set the dials on his time machine. "What is it?" he asked impatiently.

"Why is it called the TTM-6?"

"That's a good question," the professor replied as he pressed the machine's start button. He found he had to shout over the sound of the machine's spinning turbines. "TTMs 1 through 5 never returned. Good luck!"

"Never returned?" David gasped as a thick cloud of fog engulfed him.

Name _____

Professor Templeton's Time Machine

Chapter Number	Chapter Title	Authors' Names
1	_____	David Clark Yeager
2	*The Age of the Dinosaurs*	_____
3	*The Great Ice Age*	_____
4	*Exploring with Columbus*	_____
5	*Pirates Play for Keeps*	_____
6	*George Washington Slept Here*	_____
7	*One Pony Express Run Too Many*	_____
8	*Footsteps on the Moon*	_____
9	*The Year 2055* A.D.	_____
10	_____	_____

The Search for Planet Ten

Chapter One

Commander Lumennes opened the meteor shield that had protected the flight bridge during the trip from Saturn. "We are approaching the region now," she said to First Officer Bracken. "Slow to light-speed 1."

"Function completed," Bracken acknowledged. "Light-speed 1. Any sign of the tenth planet?"

"Negative," Lumennes replied as she peered through the navigation port. "Nothing yet. But a computer sampling of the space outside reveals the presence of some microscopic organic particles. They could be coming from some undiscovered planet."

Their small spacecraft had passed through the path of Pluto's orbit less than a week earlier, searching for the tenth and most mysterious planet in the solar system. Suddenly, the ship lurched forward and began spinning wildly.

"Report!" Lumennes ordered.

Bracken checked the banks of instruments before him. "We have passed through some sort of atmospheric border," he said nervously. "The gravity is pulling us toward something . . . but what?"

"That's a very good question," Lumennes replied, the fear rising in her voice. "The computer is picking up distinct life forms. There is something mysterious out there. What could it be?"

Name _____

The Search for Planet Ten

Chapter Number	Chapter Title	Authors' Names
1	_____	David Clark Yeager
2	*Encounter with a Meteor Shower*	_____
3	*A Mysterious Light*	_____
4	*Landfall on Planet Ten*	_____
5	*Damage Report*	_____
6	*Unwelcome Visitors*	_____
7	*Taken Captive*	_____
8	*Too Long on Planet Ten*	_____
9	*Escape from Planet Ten*	_____
10	_____	_____

Name _____

Robotron, Inc.

Chapter One

McGill had been on the police force for more than fifteen years. In that time, he thought, he had seen and heard just about everything. Until now, that is. Shortly after three o'clock, he had received a call from Dr. Wayne Phillopson, the director of a company called Robotron, Inc.

According to Phillopson, sixteen of Robotron's latest model robots had taken over the company by force. The robots were holding Phillopson's assistant and thirteen workers captive. The automatons were demanding to be compensated for their work and to be given annual paid vacations.

As McGill sped toward the Robotron headquarters, he noticed that the building looked quite small. Actually, Robotron, Inc., covered more than six acres. All but the front of the building was underground, buried beneath a rich green lawn.

Inspector McGill climbed from the car, chewing a piece of gum. "I suppose they know we are here."

Dr. Phillopson nodded. "They knew you were coming the minute the car passed through the gate. The Model III robot is equipped with the latest logic control circuits. That's one reason they were able to take over the plant so easily."

"Well, no bucket-of-bolts robot is going to take over a factory in my city and hold innocent workers hostage," Inspector McGill declared. "How many entrances and exits do we have here?"

Dr. Phillopson turned to the young woman standing beside him. She unrolled a set of blueprints. Guiding McGill's gaze with her forefinger, she explained, "This is the main entrance to the factory. There are two shipping docks at the end of this road and one emergency exit near the security fence. But, of course, the robots have all of those doors guarded. They won't give up until their demands are met."

"How would you know?" Inspector McGill asked skeptically.

"Andrea *should* know," Dr. Phillopson said. "She is also a Model III."

"Well, she'd better stay out of our way," Inspector McGill replied. He motioned to his men. "I guess we'll just have to do this the hard way," he said. "We're going in at sundown."

Name _____

Robotron, Inc.

Chapter Number	Chapter Title	Authors' Names
1	_____	David Clark Yeager
2	*Inspector McGill's Plan*	_____
3	*The Robots' Demands*	_____
4	*Inside the Control Room*	_____
5	*On the Assembly Line*	_____
6	*The Robots' Secret Weapon*	_____
7	*Blackout Below*	_____
8	*Countdown to Sundown*	_____
9	*The Brief Battle of Shipping Dock One*	_____
10	_____	

Name _____

The Last Woman on Earth

Chapter One

Christine reached for the pocket video-corder she had taken from the shelf of the electronics store. Although there wasn't a soul around to stop her, she still felt like a thief. She had never taken anything without paying for it before. But then, what good was money now?

Christine sat on the edge of a recently painted bench. She was alone in a park that should have been filled with the sounds of carefree children, worried mothers, barking dogs, and ice cream vendors.

But today there were no sounds. In fact, Christine hadn't heard a voice since landing her balloon that foggy night. Being the first person to fly solo over the Atlantic meant nothing if there was no one to welcome her and nothing to come home to.

She balanced the video-corder on one arm of the bench and switched it to "record" while looking into the lens. "Today is Tuesday, June 5. Or is it Wednesday, June 6?" she began. "It doesn't matter much what day it is. What's important is that it has been more than thirty days since I have seen another human being. I now know that I am probably the last human living on this planet. It is my duty to record this final chapter in the history of mankind."

Listening for the chirping of birds she knew she would never hear, Christine sat back, drew a deep breath, and continued. "I left Paris on April 29 for a transatlantic balloon flight to America. I landed near Washington, D.C., several days later. To my amazement, I discovered that the nation's capital had been abandoned. There were no signs of a war or a natural disaster. The people had simply vanished—gone without a trace. Tomorrow I will begin searching for clues to explain this incredible mystery."

Name _____

The Last Woman on Earth

Chapter Number	Chapter Title	Authors' Names
1	_____	David Clark Yeager
2	*A Tour of the White House*	_____
3	*An Unusual Trip to New York City*	_____
4	*Wandering Westward*	_____
5	*The Lonely Loop*	_____
6	*Crossing the Plains*	_____
7	*Climbing the Rockies*	_____
8	*California Castle*	_____
9	*Signs of Life?*	_____
10	_____	_____

McKenzie's Lab

Chapter One

Theodore McKenzie, better known as Test Tube to his friends and his enemies, was where he usually could be found – in the basement working on another of his great inventions.

"Ted? Ted!" his mother called from the top of the stairs. "Your cousin Milton is on the phone. He wants to know if you can come over to the park and play football with him and some of his friends."

"Play football *with* them?" Ted mumbled to himself. "Those guys are meaner than the Los Angeles Raiders. They probably are planning to use me as their football again, unless . . ." His eyes drifted back to his latest invention.

"Ted," his mother called again, "what should I tell Miltie?"

As Ted strapped himself into the McKenzie Insta-Strength Generator, he answered, "Sure, Mom, you tell Milton I'll be happy to play football with him."

"Oh, good, Teddie," she replied. "I'm glad. Getting out of that dark basement will be good for you, you'll see. And on the way home you can run a few errands for me. I'm sure you're going to have a wonderful afternoon."

Ted laughed as he switched on the generator and set the indicator on "Muscular Accelerator." "I will. I certainly will."

As Ted McKenzie turned the dial toward +10, he could feel increased strength rippling through his arms, his legs, his whole body. In seconds he was as strong as ten men, then fifteen, then twenty. Satisfied with his increased strength, Ted tried to turn off the machine, but nothing happened. The generator continued to feed power into his body.

Before long, the machine began to smoke and smolder. Ted's invention was experiencing a meltdown. Ted broke the tight metal bands he had used to strap himself to the machine and bounded up the stairs. Merely touching the basement door caused it to explode into millions of pieces under his immense strength. His invention had worked!

Name _____

McKenzie's Lab

Chapter Number	Chapter Title	Authors' Names
1	_____	David Clark Yeager
2	*A One-Man Football Team*	_____
3	*Halftime Happening*	_____
4	*To the Victor Goes a Snack*	_____
5	*Milton's Revenge*	_____
6	*Super Strength in the Supermarket*	_____
7	*Ted to the Rescue*	_____
8	*Ted Takes a Holiday*	_____
9	*Do Muscles Make the Man?*	_____
10	_____	_____

In Search of Alto Pajetan

Chapter One

"We are coming over the jump site." The Colonel had to shout to be heard over the drone of the old airplane engines. "Check your harnesses."

Crisman looked down at the Amazon forest. "I can't see anything but jungle. Are you sure Alto Pajetan, the fabled Lost City of Gold, is really down there?"

"We won't know until we get there," Dirk laughed. "But I can tell you one thing. We are jumping with an eight-day supply of food and equipment. If we don't find the city in that length of time, we'll have to hunt for lunch."

"Or end up as lunch for some alligator," the Colonel laughed. The white light above the door began flashing. "There's the signal from the pilot. It's time to jump!"

"What do you expect to find if we do locate Alto Pajetan?" Crisman asked.

The Colonel shrugged his shoulders. "Who knows what to expect? Nobody in recent history has seen the city; but legends tell us that the walls of the homes are papered with gold and that precious jewels frame the windows. If that's true, we stand a pretty good chance of getting most of the loot out of the jungle." He patted the breast pocket of his safari shirt. "I happen to have the only map showing the way back to civilization."

"And how long will it take to get back there?" Crisman gulped as he prepared to jump.

"Not too long," the Colonel shouted as Crisman floated into the air. "Just ten days or so . . . if we live, that is."

"If we live?" Crisman groaned as the wind whipped his face.

Name _____

In Search of Alto Pajetan

Chapter Number	Chapter Title	Authors' Names
1	_____	David Clark Yeager
2	*A Hard Landing*	_____
3	*Thick Vines and Strange Creatures*	_____
4	*Dark Night in a Dense Jungle*	_____
5	*A Different Kind of Welcome*	_____
6	*Alto Pajetan!*	_____
7	*One Man's Treasure*	_____
8	*Which Way Out?*	_____
9	*Will the Supplies Last?*	_____
10	_____	_____

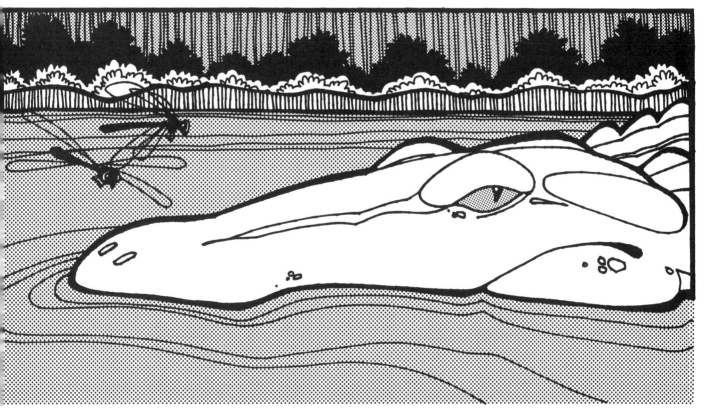

In Pursuit of the Desert Rats

Chapter One

Inspector Haibib parked the battered green Mercedes at the edge of the sand. "This is as far as we go . . . in a car," she declared, speaking with a heavy Middle Eastern accent.

Pierre Trouffelt, InterPol's most clever undercover investigator, peered through the dusty windshield at miles of blowing sand. "But we must go on. The Desert Rats are out there. I know they are. They have stolen some of France's most precious national treasures. If we don't stop them, the paintings and sculptures will be ruined."

Haibib sighed. "That may be so, my young friend. But that changes nothing. To travel farther would be foolish. That sand would certainly destroy the engine before we could go three more miles. What good would that do us? The Desert Rats would still be out there with your valuable treasures."

Trouffelt pounded the palm of his hand against the dashboard. "The Desert Rats are a plague to every civilized country on this planet. They must be apprehended, and I will do it!"

Haibib raised her hands and smiled. "I was all too afraid you were going to say that. If you are determined to catch the Desert Rats, you must travel in the same manner as they do."

"Fine, fine," Pierre agreed eagerly. "Let's get started. Now, where are the jeeps?"

Haibib laughed sardonically. "Jeeps, my friend?" She stepped from the car and began walking toward four camels being led out of the blowing sand. "The Desert Rats do not use jeeps."

Name _____

In Pursuit of the Desert Rats

Chapter Number	Chapter Title	Authors' Names
1	_____	David Clark Yeager
2	*As Stubborn as a Camel*	_____
3	*Desert Sandstorm*	_____
4	*Oasis at Last!*	_____
5	*Nomad Rendezvous*	_____
6	*A Hidden Cavern*	_____
7	*Whose Bones Are These?*	_____
8	*Hot on the Trail of the Desert Rats*	_____
9	*In the Outlaws' Camp*	_____
10	_____	_____

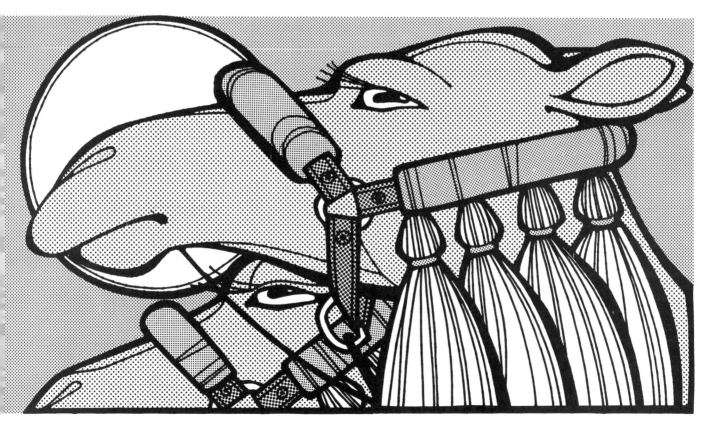

Avalanche!

Chapter One

Steve Burke looked out the large picture window. He had been the mountain manager for the past seven years. Never before had he seen quite so much snow fall in so little time.

The short wave radio at the edge of his desk crackled to life. He had been expecting this report. "Base Camp, this is Eagle's Nest. How are you desk jockeys enjoying the storm down there?"

Burke laughed nervously. "If this keeps up much longer, it'll take us until spring to dig out." Traces of worry could be heard in his voice. "I've been trying to reach you all afternoon. Is everything okay?"

As he spoke, Steve peered through a pair of high-power field glasses, trying to catch a glimpse of the Eagle's Nest station perched at the top of the Number One chairlift. His attempts were fruitless.

Steve had no way of knowing that three snow masses had been building all day and were now ready to rip down the mountainside. The Eagle's Nest ski patrol crew, led by Sven Thorgoson, had spent the last three hours shooting mortar shells at the accumulating masses, hoping to halt their growth and send them down the mountainside before they became destructive and even deadly avalanches.

The radio crackled. "We have a touchy situation up here," Sven reported. "Three big boomers are hanging right over the slopes. One false move, and tons of snow will come sliding down on top of you. It's too dangerous for us to come down. I think we'll just hole up here for the night."

There was a long pause before Steve spoke. His voice was heavy. "Sven, we have three 'ability greens' on the Rainier run. Somebody's going to have to bring them in."

Sven looked at his crew. "Ability green" was the area's name for beginning skiers. Rainier was the most difficult of the sixty-three runs in the area. To make matters worse, the Rainier run crossed right through the avalanche zone. If the boomers broke loose while members of the patrol were on the slope, they would all be buried alive.

"We copy, Base Camp," Sven said. "We'll begin the search immediately. See you at the bottom." As he signed off, Sven wondered where the missing skiers might be.

Name _____

Avalanche!

Chapter Number	Chapter Title	Authors' Names
1	_____	David Clark Yeager
2	*The Long Search Begins*	_____
3	*Darkness Falls*	_____
4	*A Cry in the Trees*	_____
5	*Snowslide*	_____
6	*Whiteout*	_____
7	*Timber Wolves*	_____
8	*Ledgetop Rescue*	_____
9	*Avalanche!*	_____
10	_____	_____

The Lost Continent

Chapter One

Betty Sarbow was listening carefully to the young explorer. She clasped her hands behind her head. Leaning back in her chair, she said, "Hundreds of people have claimed to know the location of the lost continent of Atlantis. They have all been wrong. What makes you so sure that you are right?"

Quickly spreading her charts across the wealthy investor's desk, Devreaux Bannon began her story. "Three weeks ago we picked up sonar readings here." She pointed to a remote section of ocean water.

Sarbow raised one eyebrow. "So what?"

Devreaux could see that Sarbow was losing interest. If she couldn't convince the investor to finance her next expedition, any hope of finding Atlantis would be lost. Devreaux had to speak quickly. "So, those sonar readings were of a city about the size of . . . ," she dropped her voice, making Sarbow strain to hear, ". . . New York."

"The size of New York?" Sarbow repeated, quickly sitting upright in her chair. "You mean to tell me that you actually found Atlantis? It truly exists?"

Now Sarbow was interested. "Not only is Atlantis down there," Devreaux continued in an excited whisper, "but there are people living there!"

"Underwater?" Sarbow gasped. "Can you prove it?"

Devreaux nodded. "I can if you are willing to finance my next trip," she said. "But we have to move fast. Atlantis just floats around down there like a leaf in the wind. If I don't get back there soon, it may be lost forever."

"Go! Go!" Sarbow shouted. "Just find it! I'll pay for everything. Go!"

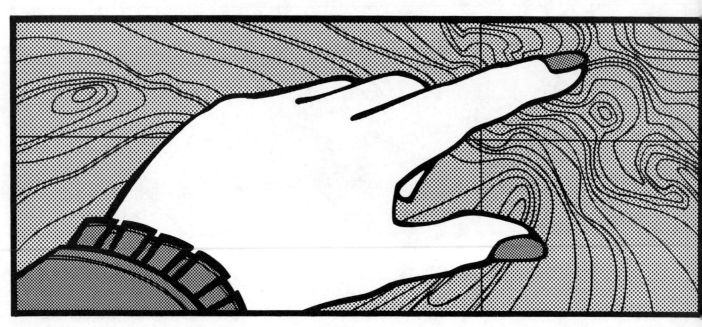

Name _____

The Lost Continent

Chapter Number	Chapter Title	Authors' Names
1	_____	David Clark Yeager
2	*Rough Waters*	_____
3	*Suspicious Sonar Signals*	_____
4	*Undersea Exploration*	_____
5	*Creatures of the Deep*	_____
6	*First Glimpse of Atlantis*	_____
7	*The City Gates*	_____
8	*An Unfriendly Welcome*	_____
9	*How Safe Is the Secret?*	_____
10	_____	_____

Name _____

The Flight of No Return

Chapter One

Cheryl Davenport, the flight engineer, leaned across the controls and said, "I'm still picking up that vibration on the main tail engine. It's beginning to worry me."

Todd Christianson, the chief test pilot, nodded. "I can feel it too," he said. "Maybe we'd better shut that engine down and bring this bird in on the two outboards."

The two had spent the past fortnight testing the Air Force's newest reconnaissance plane. The job was exciting and dangerous. They both knew that one hundred and ten thousand feet above the California desert was not the best place to develop engine trouble. But then, again, traveling at a speed of 2,220 knots left them little time to think about the fix they were in.

The plane lurched suddenly, the starboard wing dipping toward the horizon. As the plane dove toward the ground, Todd fought against the paralyzing force of gravity. It took every ounce of his strength to pull back on the stick, gradually bringing the plane out of the deadly dive.

"I can't believe this," Cheryl exclaimed. "The tail burner has come back on line. It's purring like a kitten."

"Shut it down!" Todd ordered. He felt his stomach flip and his throat grow tight. "This bird has taken off like a rocket! I can't slow it down. Another couple of minutes at this speed and she'll shatter like glass."

Davenport didn't answer. Todd turned to see his friend staring ashen-faced at the instrument panel. The airspeed continued to increase! Within a minute, they were hurtling through the air at more than 3,000 knots per hour.

"Power back! Power back!" Christianson shouted.

The plane shuddered as it slowed and then began falling toward the earth, miles off course. It was too late to do anything. The plane broke apart seconds after the automatic ejection system sent the two pilots tumbling toward a rugged mountain range.

Name _____

The Flight of No Return

Chapter Number	Chapter Title	Authors' Names
1	_____	David Clark Yeager
2	_Mountaintop Landing_	_____
3	_The Long Trek Down_	_____
4	_Dark Night in a Dead Man's Cabin_	_____
5	_A Startling Discovery_	_____
6	_Camping out Was Never Like This_	_____
7	_Search and Survival_	_____
8	_Sending Signals to the Searchers_	_____
9	_A Daring Rescue_	_____
10	_____	_____

Maphis Manor

Chapter One

"That house has been dark for more than fifteen years," Stephen explained to his cousins. "The owner came home one night and was never seen again."

Dean and Erik looked at each other and laughed. The twins had come to expect this kind of story from their cousin. Some people like to collect stamps. Stephen liked to frighten people.

"Maybe the owner is still inside," Erik laughed.

"Maybe he is," Stephen agreed, his dark eyes shining. "But no food has ever been brought to the house. Do you know anyone who can go fifteen years without eating?"

Dean and Erik shrugged their shoulders. "Maybe the guy snuck out without anyone seeing him," Erik suggested. "Or he has a secret entrance to the house," Dean added. "So what?"

"So you like mysteries, don't you?"

The twins nodded.

Stephen smiled. "Well, it just so happens that the taxes on the house have not been paid for all those years. It now belongs to the city. Tomorrow, a municipal demolition crew will begin tearing it down."

"So?" the twins asked again.

Stephen dropped to his knees. "So there is a rumor that the owner hid more than $300,000 inside that house. We have less than twenty-four hours to find it."

"Is this another one of your jokes?" Dean asked.

Stephen pointed toward the top window of the house. "Look!" he whispered excitedly.

The twins looked up just as the curtain fell.

"I guess we won't be the only people inside that house tonight!"

"Tonight?" The twins gulped, "We're going in there tonight?"

Name _____

Maphis Manor

Chapter Number	Chapter Title	Authors' Names
1	_____	David Clark Yeager
2	*Inside the Old House*	_____
3	*Creaks and Groans*	_____
4	*A Trapdoor to the Basement*	_____
5	*Footprints in the Dust*	_____
6	*A Secret Stairway*	_____
7	*Voices in the Walls*	_____
8	*A Safe in the Library*	_____
9	*Success and Capture*	_____
10	_____	_____

The Phantom

Chapter One

Falcon, Colorado, was not the biggest of towns. In fact, since the coal mine had closed down, the town wasn't much more than a wide spot in the road between Denver and Colorado Springs. But there was one thing that made Falcon famous—it was the home of the Phantom.

For more than ten years, things in Falcon that weren't nailed down had been disappearing. Nobody ever saw or heard anything. Instead, they just woke up in the morning to find that their belongings were mysteriously missing from their homes and places of business.

One poor soul even found himself homeless. Somehow, the Phantom had carried the man outside and then driven away with his six-month-old mobile home!

Nothing seemed to stop the Phantom. Sixteen town marshals had not been able to find the Phantom, much less to stop him. But Torrence DeWitt had promised to change all that. When he had been sworn in as marshal, DeWitt had vowed to catch the Phantom red-handed. And tonight was the night!

DeWitt and his deputy had spent the entire week stocking the shelves of the new hardware store. This store, DeWitt hoped, would be in business for just one night—as a trap to catch the Phantom! The marshal had placed large ads in the newspaper and on radio stations as far away as Denver. Everyone knew that the grand opening was scheduled for the following morning. The Phantom would have had to be both blind and deaf to miss all of the publicity.

It was nearly sunrise. DeWitt and his deputy were inside the darkened store, crouched behind a large display of paint, waiting for the Phantom to strike.

Suddenly, they heard noises. Before they could stand, the front door of the store flew open. A dark shadow passed through the opening. DeWitt snapped on the lights. Everything except the display of paint was gone! The Phantom had struck again.

"After him!" DeWitt shouted. "I want that man—or whatever he is—arrested!"

Name _____

The Phantom

Chapter Number	Chapter Title	Authors' Names
1	_____	David Clark Yeager
2	*Tracks*	_____
3	*A Message in the Snow*	_____
4	*Stakeout at the Falcon Garage*	_____
5	*The Phantom Is Sighted*	_____
6	*A Chase Through the Graveyard*	_____
7	*Deep in the Coal Mines*	_____
8	*DeWitt's Plan*	_____
9	*What Do You Do with a Cornered Phantom?*	_____
10	_____	_____

allon | one half gallon

interior PAINT tangerine

interior PAINT cream

Lou Dini's Last Trick

Chapter One

Normally, Cap Henderson was an unperturbable man who spoke softly. As the owner of the Magic Circus, the city's largest nightclub, he had seen many acts. But the act he had witnessed tonight was enough to make him pace nervously about and declare loudly, "I don't know how he did it. I just don't know *how* he did it!"

Detective Rousseau put his hat on the table, took out a notebook, and said, "Why don't you take it from the top?"

Cap took a long, slow breath and then began. "Two days ago this guy named Lou Dini comes in. He claims to be some big magician from Canada."

"Was he looking for a job?" Rousseau asked, writing in the small notebook as he spoke.

Cap nodded. "He couldn't have picked a better time. My main act for the weekend didn't show. I needed some entertainment and fast!"

"So you gave him the job?" Rousseau anticipated.

"I sure did," Cap said. "Dini opened the early show on Friday night. He wasn't just good. He was fantastic! He had more tricks up his sleeve than a poker dealer has aces."

Cap took a sip of water before continuing. "Tonight, Dini comes up with this crazy idea. He wants me to put $50,000 in cash on stage with him. He's going to make it disappear during the show."

"And you went along with the plan?" Rousseau probed. "Fifty grand is a lot of money."

"You're telling me," Cap moaned. "But it sounded like a great publicity stunt. Besides, security was tight. I had four armed guards standing over the money all the time."

"Yet the money disappeared anyway?"

Cap nodded. "The money and Lou Dini. During the act, all of this smoke began rising from the floor of the stage. When it had cleared, Dini and the money were gone—like magic!"

Rousseau flipped closed the cover of his notebook. "I don't believe in magic," he said, "just facts. This Lou Dini had better not look over his shoulder. I'm hot on his trail." Rousseau walked to the stage, carefully looking at the floor. "Yes sir, hot on his trail."

Name _____

Lou Dini's Last Trick

Chapter Number	Chapter Title	Authors' Names
1	_____	David Clark Yeager
2	*A Closer Look at the Scene of the Crime*	_____
3	*A Stage Floor Door*	_____
4	*An Underground Exit*	_____
5	*Clues Among the Costumes*	_____
6	*A Suspect on the Lighting Bridge*	_____
7	*Lou Dini Returns*	_____
8	*Up in Smoke*	_____
9	*On the Money Trail*	_____
10	_____	_____

The Gold Miner's Secret

Chapter One

"This place really gives me the creeps," Anthony complained as he pulled his jacket out of the backpack. "Are you sure we want to cover this story?"

Heather laughed easily. "Don't tell me the award-winning photographer is afraid of a rustic old ghost town. I thought you wanted to be in on all of the action."

"I did. I do. But don't you think we could gather our facts better in the daylight? A nice warm restaurant sounds pretty good right about now."

"It'll have to wait," Heather replied matter-of-factly as she parked the jeep near the abandoned saloon. "Besides, if we get lucky, we may have this story wrapped up by midnight. According to the legend, the lost miner shows up every year on this date. Old timers believe that he has come to check on his mine, which is hidden somewhere near this town."

"Are you sure this is the right place," Anthony asked, "and the right town? We may be in the wrong place at the wrong time."

"Impossible," Heather snapped. "This is the date. It's now or never." She turned off her flashlight and pointed to a strange glowing light at the edge of town. "I think our guest of honor has just made his appearance," she whispered. "Let's follow him."

Name _____

The Gold Miner's Secret

Chapter Number	Chapter Title	Authors' Names
1	_____	David Clark Yeager
2	*A Glow in the Graveyard*	_____
3	*The Hangman's Gallows*	_____
4	*Following Footprints to the Old Saloon*	_____
5	*A Chase into the Church*	_____
6	*A Ghostly Guest in the Grand Hotel*	_____
7	*More Than Shoes in the Blacksmith's Shop*	_____
8	*A Trail into the Hills*	_____
9	*Furtive Peek at a Hidden Mine*	_____
10	_____	_____

The Case of the Missing Mummy

Chapter One

Professor Margolis hurried across the airport tarmac toward the terminal. She still could not believe her good fortune.

For fifteen years, she had searched the desert. Beneath the unrelenting Egyptian sun, she had hunted for the lost tomb of Ank-Hamen, a great pharaoh of ancient Egypt.

Most of the time, the search had seemed endless. But then, just nine weeks ago, Professor Margolis had stumbled onto something extraordinary. Beneath centuries of sand and rubble, she had found a staircase. That staircase led to the most magnificent tomb the professor had ever seen. It had been perfectly preserved, untouched for centuries.

The sarcophagus found in the tomb was being shipped to the professor's laboratory for closer examination. But both the mummy and its stone case were rare Egyptian treasures. In just ten days, they had to be returned to the government museum in Cairo.

The chief customs inspector walked over to the sarcophagus. He was accompanied by Mohammed Ali Sabir, the curator of the Egyptian museum.

"We must certify that this shipment contains the mummy of Ank-Hamen," the inspector said to Professor Margolis. "Mr. Sabir has agreed to help us do that."

Professor Margolis nodded. "Certainly. I understand." She stepped aside as the customs inspector opened the three locks that secured the specially built crate that had protected the sarcophagus during shipment.

Mohammed Ali Sabir gasped. He stared down at a mound of dirt. "Ank-Hamen has been stolen," he shouted.

The professor shook her head in disbelief. "That's impossible," she declared. "I was with the shipment all the way from Egypt. It was never out of my sight until just now. How could Ank-Hamen have been stolen? And who would do such a thing?"

Sabir clenched his fist as he watched a small white delivery truck speed away. "I think we may have our answer. The driver of that truck is none other than Abdul Malad, a thief who specializes in stealing priceless museum pieces to sell to wealthy clients. We must stop him!"

Name _____

The Case of the Missing Mummy

Chapter Number	Chapter Title	Authors' Names
1	_____	David Clark Yeager
2	*Who is Abdul Malad?*	_____
3	*Where Would a Man Like Malad Hide a Mummy?*	_____
4	*Sabir Searches for a Sarcophagus*	_____
5	*Professor Margolis Aids the Search*	_____
6	*The Mummy Went Thataway*	_____
7	*Ransom for a Mummy*	_____
8	*Malad's Mistake*	_____
9	*Ank-Hamen's Homecoming*	_____
10	_____	_____

Mrs. Begilia's Vegetable Garden

Chapter One

The three boys crouched behind the picket fence. Their view was partly blocked by the biggest tomato plants in the entire county. "There she is," Aaron whispered hoarsely.

They watched as Mrs. Begilia moved slowly through her garden, talking to each of the plants as if it were a child.

"That's weird," Andy said, breaking into a laugh.

Danny clasped his hand over Andy's mouth. "Be quiet, will you? We'll never find out how she does it if she chases us away."

Everyone in town knew that Mrs. Begilia's garden was unusual. Each year she was able to produce the largest vegetables in the county—perhaps in the entire country. Just how she did it was her most closely guarded secret, a secret that some people were willing to pay for.

Aaron Donner, his brother Andy, and their next-door neighbor Danny Archer were always broke. Finding out how Mrs. Begilia grew a bunch of carrots seemed like an easy way to pick up a little spending money.

The three crawled along the edge of the fence, watching as Mrs. Begilia walked among her plants. She stopped beside a large cornstalk and said, "How is my young corn this morning?"

"Look, look!" Andy said suddenly. "The cornstalk is moving! It's answering her question. Unbelievable!"

"Impossible," Danny responded. He brushed aside the tomato leaves to get a clearer look at the garden. Andy was right. The cornstalk was bent over. It looked as if it were whispering into Mrs. Begilia's right ear.

"Oh?" Mrs. Begilia said, suddenly turning toward where the boys were hiding. "We have visitors, do we? Why don't you show them into the shed?"

The frightened boys turned to run, but they were too late.

Name _____

Mrs. Begilia's Vegetable Garden

Chapter Number	Chapter Title	Authors' Names
1	_____	David Clark Yeager
2	*Taken Captive*	_____
3	*A Night in Mrs. Begilia's Toolshed*	_____
4	*A Remarkable Discovery*	_____
5	*The Plot Thickens*	_____
6	*A Way Out*	_____
7	*Recapture in the Bean Field*	_____
8	*Things Could Not Be as Bad as They Seem*	_____
9	*Getting a Message to the Outside World*	_____
10	_____	_____

The Luck o' the Irish

Chapter One

Carl Dillinger pounded his fist on the flower shop counter. "I want a plant, and I want it fast," he declared.

The elderly florist shuffled in from the back room. "The saints be with ya, laddie," he said in a lilting Irish accent. "What kind of plant would ya be lookin' for?"

Dillinger grumbled. "I don't care. It's for my secretary. Today's her birthday. A plant is a plant. Just make it fast and cheap."

"I think I'll be having just the thing," the proprietor winked. He pulled a large green plant from beneath the counter. "Perhaps a nice shamrock plant?"

"Whatever, whatever," Dillinger said hurriedly. "How much is it?"

The florist smiled oddly. "I'd be thinkin' you need the plant more than me. The luck o' the Irish is in that plant. No charge."

Dillinger laughed cynically. "With prices like that, I don't know how you stay in business. But as they always say, a fool and his money are soon parted. This must be my lucky day."

The proprietor nodded. "It may be your lucky day, but remember, laddie, luck must be used wisely."

Dillinger picked up the shamrock and headed out the door. He had almost reached his car when a gust of wind blew across the parking lot. He watched as the wind lifted a billfold from the top of a woman's shopping bag. The wallet hit the ground, and the contents spilled out. The woman did not notice as a fifty dollar bill landed under the front tire of her car.

Carl waited until the woman had picked up her wallet and gotten into her car. Then, he reached down for the money. "I guess the luck o' the Irish really is with me," he laughed.

As he greedily grabbed the money, the car suddenly rocked forward, pinning his fingers beneath the tire. Dillinger cried for help. Then he remembered the florist's parting words: "Luck must be used wisely."

Name _____

The Luck o' the Irish

Chapter Number	Chapter Title	Authors' Names
1	_____	David Clark Yeager
2	*What Are Your Fingers Doing Under My Tire?*	_____
3	*Happy Birthday to You*	_____
4	*The Secretary's Sudden Shamrock Allergy*	_____
5	*New Home for an Old Plant*	_____
6	*Wishing for Wealth*	_____
7	*Marvelous Monetary Misadventure*	_____
8	*Money Can't Buy Happiness*	_____
9	*Money Can Buy Trouble*	_____
10	_____	_____

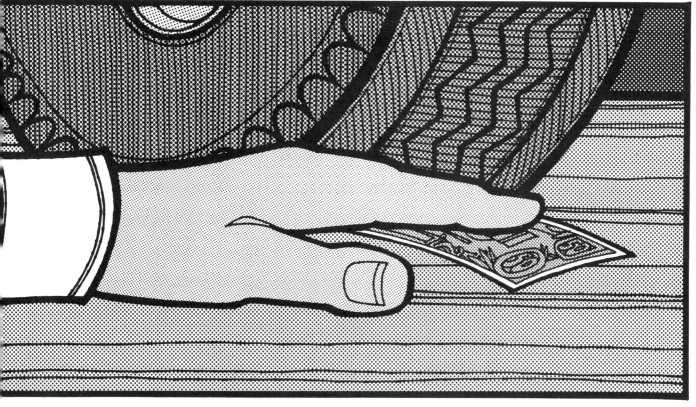

The Woman Who Could See Tomorrow

Chapter One

The Widow Washington's family sat in a tight circle in her darkened living room. The attorney arrived carrying his briefcase. After what seemed forever, he set the case down and opened it.

"We are gathered here for the reading of Mrs. Washington's last will and testament," the lawyer said to her relatives. "There is just one condition."

Walter Washington, the widow's nephew, leaned forward in his chair. "And what is that one condition?"

The lawyer looked at each of the six people assembled in the room. "You must decide now, *before* I read the will, whether or not you will accept what Mrs. Washington has left you."

Andrea Washington, the widow's cousin, cackled. "Now isn't that just like her? How could I possibly know whether or not I *want* what she left me *before* I know *what* she left me?"

The attorney shrugged his shoulders. "I'm only doing as she asked. Do you all agree to this condition?"

"Oh, of course we do," Andrea responded impatiently. "Let's get on with it."

The lawyer looked at each person, waiting for his or her permission to begin. They all nodded nervously. "Very good," he said as he tore off the seal on the will. "Andrea Washington, we will begin with you."

Andrea squealed with delight and leaned forward in her chair, expecting the best.

The lawyer's voice was quiet as he handed Andrea a small bottle. "To Andrea Washington, a relentless gossip and snoop, I leave one gift: the ability to see into tomorrow. Use this potion carefully, for you may not like what you see."

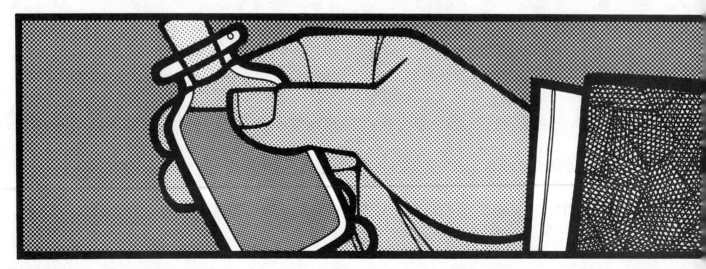

Name _____

The Woman Who Could See Tomorrow

Chapter Number	Chapter Title	Authors' Names
1	_____	David Clark Yeager
2	*Other Unusual Legacies*	_____
3	*Andrea's Anxious Moments*	_____
4	*Putting the Potion to Work*	_____
5	*First Glimpse of the Future*	_____
6	*Confusion and Clairvoyance*	_____
7	*An Unpleasant Vision*	_____
8	*To Tell or Not to Tell*	_____
9	*A Timely Warning*	_____
10	_____	_____

Faster Than a Speeding Bullet

Chapter One

Maynard Goodwell stood in front of the mirror. He had been on the Pendleton Power Diet for three weeks, and nothing had happened. He was still Maynard the Muffin. He wasn't any taller, any stronger, or any faster. But most distressing was the fact that he wasn't the super hero the diet plan promised he would become.

The Pendleton Power Diet, he decided, was a fraud, just like all of the others he had tried. But this time he wasn't going to let them get away with it. He dressed quickly, picked up his last can of Power Diet Formula, and stormed to the small shop where he had made his purchase.

Grasping one door handle in each clenched fist, Maynard threw open the french front doors and simultaneously declared, "I want my money back. This stuff is worthless."

Max Pendleton, inventor of the Pendleton Power Diet, looked up from his desk. "Worthless?" he asked, shocked.

Maynard slid the can across the desk. "Worthless. I followed the instructions, and nothing happened. I am *exactly* the same wimpy person I was twenty-one days ago."

Max fumbled through his records. "Maynard, isn't it?" he asked. "Ah, yes, here it is. Why Maynard, nothing should have happened yet."

Maynard, who was about to begin shouting again, stopped short. "Nothing should have happened?"

"Nothing," Max smiled. "At least until noon. According to the instructions, you must take the formula for twenty-one *full* days. The twenty-first day is not over until noon today. You still have twenty-three minutes to wait."

Maynard sat outside Max's shop, looking at his watch. The minutes passed like an eternity. Finally, noon arrived. As the bells of city hall chimed in the background, Maynard could feel himself changing. After a lifetime of waiting, Maynard's ultimate dream had come true. Maynard was a super hero!

Name _____

Faster Than a Speeding Bullet

Chapter Number	Chapter Title	Authors' Names
1	_____	David Clark Yeager
2	*Stronger Than Fiction*	_____
3	*Maynard's First Heroic Adventure*	_____
4	*Maynard Senses Danger*	_____
5	*Maynard Saves the Subway*	_____
6	*Max and His Formula Disappear*	_____
7	*Maynard Saves Max*	_____
8	*Maynard Makes a Mistake*	_____
9	*The Power Fails*	_____
10	_____	_____

A Night in Pompeii

Chapter One

Donna Donovan stepped off the tour bus and looked around. The walls of the ancient city towered before her. Tourists jostled one another, snapping pictures of Vesuvius, one of the world's most famous volcanoes.

"I've wanted to come here all of my life," Donna told the large woman standing next to her. "Did you know that Mount Vesuvius erupted exactly two thousand years ago today? Wouldn't it have been exciting to live in those days?"

The large woman stared at Donna from beneath the rim of a wide, floppy hat. "Nut," she muttered as she pushed two small children out of her way.

Donna turned her attention back toward the sleeping volcano. As she did so, she noticed a narrow path leading toward the still-standing walls of the ancient city of Pompeii. How odd, she thought, that no one else had noticed the path. After hesitating for a moment, Donna shrugged her shoulders, and then began to follow it.

Donna had walked only a few yards when, looking over her shoulder, she noticed that the tour buses and the crowds were no longer visible. All she could see were the sides of the mountain and the walls of the city. It was as if she had stepped back in time!

Donna's attention was again drawn to the path when she heard the sound of horses hooves against its rough stone surface. The rider pulled up short, out of breath.

"Why are you heading for the city?" the rider asked. "Haven't you felt the rumblings?"

Donna smiled. "Is this some sort of recreation of the past?"

The rider looked more closely at Donna before speaking. "You are not from Pompeii, are you? Wherever you are from, heed my warning: The city is not safe for living creatures. You would do well to flee." Without another word, the rider sped on.

Name _____

A Night in Pompeii

Chapter Number	Chapter Title	Authors' Names
1	_____	David Clark Yeager
2	*On the Path to Pompeii*	_____
3	*From Farming Hamlet to Bustling Metropolis*	_____
4	*Inside the Ancient City*	_____
5	*Temples, Theaters, and Townhouses*	_____
6	*Warning Rumbles from a Restless Mountain*	_____
7	*Fire Fills the Sky*	_____
8	*A Rain of Cinder and Ash*	_____
9	*The Path Rediscovered*	_____
10	_____	_____

How to Bind Your Novel

1. Your novel should have a cover, endpapers, and enough inside pages to accommodate a title page, a table of contents, and all of the chapters you have written. Decide how many inside pages you will need.

2. Divide this number of pages by four to determine how many sheets of 11-by-17-inch paper you will need.

3. Obtain this number of sheets of plain white paper plus two sheets of 12-by-18-inch colored construction paper.

4. Trim the construction paper to measure 11 inches by 17 inches.

5. Lay all of the sheets of plain white paper atop both sheets of construction paper.

6. Fold the stacked sheets in half as shown.

7. Using a sewing machine, stitch the white paper and the construction paper together along the fold, leaving at least 3 inches of thread free at each end.

8. Tie off and clip the thread at both ends.

9. Cut two pieces of cardboard 9 inches by 11½ inches.

10. Cut a large sheet of butcher, shelf, or wrapping paper to measure 13½ inches by 20½ inches.

11. Glue the two cardboard pieces side by side and ½ inch apart on the large sheet of paper.

12. Trim the corners of the paper, fold the paper over the cardboard, carefully mitering the corners, and apply glue to hold the paper in place.

13. Spread glue evenly on the outside sheet of construction paper and press it against the inside of the cardboard cover.

14. Copy your novel into your bound book by hand or type your novel carefully so that the blocks of type can be cut apart and pasted in your book. In either case, remember to leave plenty of room for illustrations!

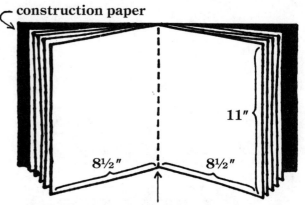

construction paper

11″

8½″   8½″

Fold and sew down middle.

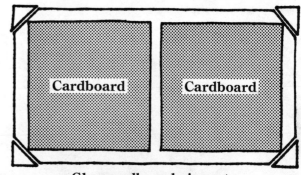

Cardboard   Cardboard

Glue cardboard pieces to paper and trim corners.

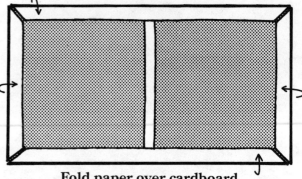

Fold paper over cardboard and glue in place.